Comprehension Strategies
for Middle Grade Learners

A Handbook for Content Area Teachers

Charlotte Rose Sadler
Gwinnett County Public Schools
Lawrenceville, Georgia, USA

INTERNATIONAL
Reading Association
800 BARKSDALE ROAD, PO BOX 8139
NEWARK, DE 19714-8139, USA
www.reading.org

The International Reading Association attempts, through its publications, to provide a forum for a wide spectrum of opinions on reading. This policy permits divergent viewpoints without implying the endorsement of the Association.

Director of Publications   Joan M. Irwin
Editorial Director, Books and Special Projects   Matthew W. Baker
Senior Editor, Books and Special Projects   Tori Mello Bachman
Permissions Editor   Janet S. Parrack
Production Editor   Shannon Benner
Editorial Assistant   Tyanna L. Collins
Publications Manager   Beth Doughty
Production Department Manager   Iona Sauscermen
Supervisor, Electronic Publishing   Anette Schütz-Ruff
Senior Electronic Publishing Specialist   Cheryl J. Strum
Electronic Publishing Specialist   Lynn Harrison
Proofreader   Charlene M. Nichols

Project Editors   Matthew W. Baker and Shannon Benner

Cover Design   Sam Gibson

Library of Congress Cataloging-in-Publication Data
Sadler, Charlotte Rose, 1963–
    Comprehension strategies for middle grade learners : a handbook for content area teachers / Charlotte Rose Sadler.
        p.   cm.
Includes bibliographical references.
    ISBN 0-87207-292-4
1. Reading comprehension.   2. Reading (Middle School).   I. Title.
    LB1050.45 .S33 2001
    428.4'071'2—dc21

2001003584
Printed in Canada

Contents

Acknowledgments

I would like to thank the following people:

Dr. Bill Hammond, DeKalb County Schools—for believing, encouraging, and making this book possible. Your support has been appreciated.

Dr. Kathleen McKenzie, my sister—for providing strategies and for your constant willingness to read, reread, make suggestions, and assist me in completing this book.

Rosalind McIntyre—for your support, your suggestions, and your contribution of strategies.

Dr. Dianne Mancus—for taking time to assist me in contributing additional strategies.

Julie Pederson—for taking the time to provide me with an excellent strategy long distance!

Eric D. Sadler, my husband—for being supportive throughout the writing, rewriting, editing, rewriting, draft corrections, rewriting, etc. Thank you for everything....

Introduction

As educators, we strive to prepare students to become successful, contributing members of society. Reading is a vital part of this preparedness. It is more than matching sounds with letters or learning sight words; reading involves comprehension—understanding what is read, what is meant, what is implied. When students have comprehension difficulties, the task of text instruction becomes increasingly complicated for educators. How can students learn from text if they cannot understand their assigned readings? This issue can be approached from different perspectives depending on the grade level of the students.

For teachers of middle school students there are several issues to consider. By the time students have reached middle school, they are expected to read and comprehend grade-level texts. Many middle school teachers are uncertain how to approach instructing students who have difficulties with text comprehension. They may assume that this is the job of the reading teacher, or they may feel they do not have the skills to teach reading. In reality, we are all reading teachers. If students have a problem reading or comprehending the text we have assigned, it is our job to assist them.

This book offers 56 strategies for middle-grade learners, with descriptions, discussions, and examples of how these strategies can be used in different content areas. Included with each strategy is a description of the strategy and its uses, content area examples, and suggestions for assessment. Depending on the student reading differences in the classroom, these strategies can be used with individuals, small groups, or the entire class.

The strategies have been divided into six sections based on their primary goal. "Checking for Understanding" features strategies that will assist you in assessing the level of students' comprehension and show how to help students increase their comprehension. Awareness of comprehension level is important to you and to the students in your classroom. Many of these strategies require students to share the information they have learned with you or with another student. The student is able to use these strategies to assess the information he or she has comprehended in a format that is not strictly reading questions and writing out answers.

"Fostering Cooperative Learning" contains strategies that improve the comprehension of students working with partners or small groups. These strategies are especially useful in situations in which you believe a student will increase his or her comprehension with peer support. The strategies can be used with small groups or an entire class.

"Connecting to Previous Knowledge" provides strategies that allow readers to connect the information they are reading to knowledge or interests they already have. These strategies are especially useful in motivating students and creating interest in new topics.

"Improving Organization" provides strategies for helping students to organize material in a way that will improve their comprehension. These strategies incorporate the use of outlines and charts.

"Promoting Independent Learning" offers strategies that students can learn and apply independently in numerous situations. The main focus is teaching the necessary steps of each strategy so students will be able to use a particular strategy independently when needed. These strategies provide students with a way to approach a particular concept, word, section of text, or to question and break down the information into steps, which will increase their levels of understanding.

"Teaching to Learning Style" contains strategies that specifically focus on one or more mode of learning (visual, auditory, tactile, etc.). Because students learn in a variety of ways, you can use these strategies to help students with particular learning styles who have strength in a particular modality.

The strategies presented in this collection not only will assist students with reading comprehension difficulties, but they also will enhance students' learning experiences through a variety of modes and methods that may encourage the reluctant reader and enrich the experience of the enthusiastic reader. This variety gives students the opportunity to gain comprehension through the mode or strategy that best suits them individually.

Checking for Understanding

Clink and Clunk

Click and Clunk is an excellent means to assess what information the students have learned and what information needs to be covered in more depth. This strategy helps students recognize the information they do not understand, and assists them in getting the information they need. It motivates students as they attempt to increase the information they understand ("clinks") and decrease what they do not understand ("clunks").

Procedure

Have students create two columns on their paper and label them "Clink" and "Clunk." Next, have the students read a passage, then list what they really understand (Clink) and what they do not understand (Clunk). As a group, discuss the "Clunks" and try to clarify the information. This can be done through direct teacher instruction or by allowing students who understand the issue to explain it to the class.

Language Arts
Topic: Parts of Speech

Clink	Clunk
nouns	adverbs
verbs	prepositions
adjectives	interjections
pronouns	

Social Studies
Topic: Roman Republic

Clink	Clunk
dictator	plebeian
republic	patrician
veto	consul
why it collapsed	why a republic was formed

Science

Clink	Clunk
concentrated	saturated
matter	diluted
	colloid
	solvent

Math
Topic: Equations and Inequalities

Clink	Clunk
solving equations	polynomials
operations	function notation
	variables

Assessment

After covering the material, discuss the Clink-Clunk list again to see if all the "Clunk" items can be moved to "Clink." Those terms in the "Clunk" column that are clearly understood can be moved to the "Clink" column and any terms remaining in the "Clunk" column should be explained further.

Vaughn & Klingner, 1999

Cued Retelling

Cued retelling is when a partner helps to prompt with retelling of a story. Having a prepared list of important information helps students recognize those things they should cover. After time, students may be able to generate their own list of items that should be covered during a retelling.

Procedure

Prepare a list of important information that you would like the students to know. Have students read the story or text independently, then have students work with a partner and retell the information they have just read. The student who is listening should have a copy of the information you would like known to ensure that all points have been mentioned.

Language Arts
- Read a story dealing with animals or human experiences. Students seem to be able to relate to these topics, which will make retelling easier.
- Distribute a sheet for summarizing/cues (e.g., character description, motivation, plot, setting, main topic, vocabulary).
- Pair students and ask them to follow procedures.

Social Studies
- Read a section of text on Egypt.
- Distribute sheet for summarizing/cues (e.g., how Egyptians lived, their religion, the climate, pharaohs, gods, etc.).
- Pair students and ask them to follow procedures.

Assessment

Use teacher questioning, observation of retelling, worksheets, or quizzes to determine comprehension. Students should be able to correctly retell 80% of a story or text. If they are unable to do so, they should reread the text (possibly aloud with a partner), then attempt the paired procedure again. Students who are still having difficulties should try this strategy with a shorter or simpler text selection.

Discussion

Although this seems like a basic and simple strategy, the depth and level of discussion can contribute to comprehension and can incorporate other skills, such as communication and organization. With Discussion, students attend to vocabulary as they come to it instead of prior to reading the selection. This strategy allows you to check for understanding by providing immediate feedback from the students rather than waiting for written feedback. If students are having difficulty understanding the selection, you may need to supply additional information to increase the students' level of understanding.

Procedure

Begin by reading a selection aloud or independently. The class should then discuss what is important in the particular piece, such as character motivation. Encourage students to voice their opinions and support their viewpoints.

Language Arts
Discuss the motivation of the characters and why they do what they do. Read "Your Three Minutes Are Up" by Ellen Conford and ask, Do you think Libby's father is being fair? Why does Libby feel as she does? What does *inalienable* mean? How did Libby's point of view change after Mark's call?

Social Studies
Discuss Africa's first people and ask, How did early Africans get their food? What civilizations arose along the Nile River? What do you know about Ancient Egypt? What are some achievements of ancient Egyptian and Nubian civilizations?

Science
Discuss the nature of light and ask, What is reflection? How does light travel? What material does light move through the fastest? What are the differences between opaque, transparent, and translucent?

Assessment

Through observation and questioning during the discussion, determine students' level of comprehension. Refer to the text as needed to support the discussion.

Alvermann, Young, Weaver, Hinchman, Moore, Phelps, Thrash, & Zalewski, 1996

Games

After covering the set material for a particular unit in a subject, use games as instructional tools to review the information and to check for understanding. Students tend to enjoy this strategy and learn more than if they were taking notes and answering questions. They are more motivated and involved in their learning.

Procedure

Games can be as simple as dividing the class into teams and asking questions, awarding points for correct answers. You may choose to use a "Jeopardy" format with more structured information presented on the board. Another popular format is "Who Wants to Be a Millionaire." Use a quick initial round and three simple rounds before declaring a winner and beginning again.

Language Arts
"Who Wants to Be a Millionaire" Format

Question	Answers			
Who was the main character?	A. Libby	B. Stacey	C. Mother	D. Mark
In the story, Libby was	A. selfish	B. jealous	C. sensitive	D. quiet

Social Studies
"Jeopardy" Format

Question	Answer
The average weather of a place over several years	What is climate?
The total number of people in a given area	What is population?

Science
"Jeopardy" Format

Question	Answer
The three states of matter	What are solid, liquid, gas?
The stages of metamorphosis of a butterfly	What are egg, larva, pupa, adult?

Math
Read word problems and have short-answer competitions with simple problem solving. The first group with a correct answer gets 5 points; all groups that get a correct answer get 3 points.

Assessment

Evaluate answers to determine comprehension. If one team is unable to answer a question, allow another team an attempt to answer. If no one can answer the question correctly, share the answer with the students and use the same question at a later time.

Bean & Zigmond, 1994

Language Arts

Social Studies

Science

Get the Gist

This strategy helps students to focus on the main idea in a passage. It also gives them the opportunity to learn how others think as they state their ideas and reasons. This allows you to check students' understanding of summarization and to determine if they can correctly identify the main idea.

Procedure

Have the students read a short passage, then discuss with them what the passage was about. Ask individual students to identify if the passage was mainly about a person, place, or thing, and decide what was most important. Ask the class members if they agree. If not, have others explain what they feel was most important. After discussion, have each student write one sentence summarizing what the class decided was the main idea.

Language Arts
Topic: Adjectives as a part of speech
Passage about: thing (words)
Summarizing sentence: Adjectives are words that are used to describe nouns.
(This activity can be done with stories, but limit it to a couple of paragraphs at a time.)

Social Studies
Topic: Rome's beginnings
Passage about: people
Summarizing sentence: We do not know a great deal about the original founders of Rome; however, we know that they used many ideas from the people they defeated, such as the Greeks.

Science
Topic: Glacier
Passage about: thing
Summarizing sentence: Glaciers are huge masses of moving snow and ice that change the land by scraping, deposition, and erosion.

Assessment

Evaluate the summary sentence to determine if students were able to state the main idea.

Swanson & De La Paz, 1998; Vaughn & Klingner, 1999

Interactive Read-Alouds

This strategy involves reading text aloud and posing questions throughout the reading to involve students in the learning process. Through guided questions, students are able to share their knowledge with one another. This is an uncomplicated means of determining students' level of understanding, because no materials are necessary and you can receive immediate feedback.

Procedure

In order to be effective, be prepared with planned questions to stimulate discussion. It is also important to anticipate when it may be necessary to build background knowledge for the students. Read a text aloud and pose questions throughout the reading. Invite brief interactions with the students, who may respond personally or interpersonally.

Language Arts
Read a few paragraphs in a story, then ask topic-specific questions such as, What can you tell me about the main character at this time? What is the main idea of this passage?

Social Studies
Read about climate and vegetation in the desert. Ask questions such as, What makes a cactus able to survive in the desert? What causes an oasis to exist?

Science
Read about prisms and ask questions such as, What causes the colors to form as light passes through a prism? How is this related to a rainbow?

Math
Read word problems, then ask questions such as, What is the problem asking you to do? Which operations do you need to use? How should you set up this problem?

Assessment

Use teacher observation, discussion, and correct responses to questions to determine comprehension. Teacher observation should include monitoring the involvement of individual students and their responses. Discussion can be used to determine students' level of comprehension by assessing their responses. Encourage responses from students who appear off task. If students do not respond correctly, provide additional information and refer back to the text in order to reexamine the passage.

Barrentine, 1996

Page and Paragraph

This strategy will assist you in checking for understanding by allowing students to respond to questions after reading short passages. It helps students to get started with reading a section and allows them to see how larger sections of text can be broken down into smaller parts. This is generally used as a start-up strategy to help the entire class begin to focus on the text.

Procedure

Begin by reading aloud a portion of the selection. Then allow students to read silently. Students who have difficulties comprehending while reading silently may continue oral reading in a small group without disrupting the entire class.

Language Arts
Read the first page of a story aloud. Have students read a specified amount silently. Stop and assess comprehension through discussion and questions. Repeat the process throughout the story and allow students who need to read aloud to continue to do so in small groups.

Social Studies/Science
Choose a text selection. Read one paragraph aloud in the first section. Allow students to finish the section silently. Walk around and assess. Allow those who need to continue reading aloud to do so.

Assessment

Monitor the involvement of individual students and their responses. Discussion can be used to determine students' level of comprehension by assessing their responses after reading. Teachers should encourage responses from students who appear off task. Students should correctly respond to 80% of the questions during a discussion or quiz. Assist students who need to continue to read aloud by pairing them with other readers.

Paraphrasing/Summarizing

This strategy involves reading a paragraph or short section, putting the information aside, asking questions about the main idea and important details, then putting the main idea and details into your own words in complete sentences. This is a strategy that is necessary not only for comprehension, but also for reports and term papers. It assesses students' comprehension because they cannot rely on the author's wording.

Procedure

Model this strategy before the students attempt it. Follow these steps:

- Explain to students the skill of summarizing, or providing a brief description of the information that was covered.
- Model summarizing short passages.
- Give students guided practice.
- Have the students individually practice summarizing. Check to ensure understanding.
- Extend the concept and have students use it on their own.

Students should be encouraged to make their summaries informative, yet brief. Use a portion of text that has already been studied, then try it with unfamiliar text.

Language Arts
Read: *The men labored day after day preparing for the flood. There were numerous times when they would work for 16 hours without a break.*
Own words: The men worked for days—often for 16 hours without a break—as they prepared for the flood.

Social Studies
Read: *All the streams and rivers in a major drainage basin form a river system. The Mississippi River system drains about one third of the United States.*
Own words: The Mississippi River is a major river system, consisting of numerous streams and rivers, that drains approximately one third of the United States.

Science
Read: *The electricity supplied by a battery flows in one direction. This is called a direct current.*
Own words: A direct current is when electricity flows in one direction—like in a battery.

(continued)

Gunning, 1996; Katims & Harris, 1997; Vacca & Vacca, 1989

Assessment

Determine comprehension through discussion and evaluation of paraphrased statements. Discussion can be used to determine students' level of comprehension by assessing their responses after reading. Encourage responses from students who appear off task. Students should correctly respond to 80% of the questions during a discussion. Evaluate the paraphrased statements and determine if the students have correctly summarized the passage. If students have difficulties with this, have other students share their paraphrasing or model paraphrasing to assist them.

Problem of the Week (POW)

This strategy is especially useful in mathematics, but can also be used in grammar, to gain insight into the thought process that students use in their problem solving. Because this is done each week, it is easier to determine the progress of the students and to decide what additional problem-solving strategies may need to be taught.

Procedure

Each week, place a problem on the board. Give students specific steps to follow:

- Restate the problem in their own words.
- Describe the procedure they used (who helped and what was tried).
- Describe what was learned and if the concept had been seen before.
- Give the answer; determine if it is reasonable and if there is more than one possible answer.
- Make certain at least two adults or peers have proofread the paper before it is turned in.

Language Arts
Write: *She was disgusted I really hate it Mary said when we don't have any money therefore I think we should wait until we save our allowance before we go out*
Have students state what needs to be done with punctuation. Discuss why each type of punctuation is used.

Math
Word problem: Four seventh graders went to the movies. Mary had $7, Ben had $11, Jen had $6, and Lynn had $12. Tickets cost $3.50 each. Each person bought a soda for $1.00, popcorn for $.75, and a candy bar for $.50. Ben bought two posters for $3.00 each. How much money was spent? How much money does each person have left? What is the total amount left? If the amount left were divided equally, how much would each person get?

Assessment

Evaluate the final answer to determine if it gives a reasonable explanation for solving the problem.

Fuentes, 1998

Retelling

Retelling is powerful because it requires a deep understanding of a passage. This strategy is more detailed than summarizing in that it asks students to tell what the story or text is about by using his or her own words. The text cannot be "summed up" in a few sentences. Students must be aware of details and sequence. This strategy can be used with an entire class, but there will be more participation with the use of partners.

Procedure

Begin by introducing what retelling is and giving an example. Explain that retelling will only focus on the main elements. (In fiction, the main elements include story problem, main plot, resolution of the problem, and ending; in nonfiction, the main elements include main idea, details, sequential presentation, and description.) Give guided practice using a story that has already been read. Students should be allowed to work in pairs to read and retell the passages. Perhaps give the students notecards so they can write two or three ideas to help them summarize.

Language Arts
Use this activity with stories, poems, or grammar rules. Students read and tell the main points to their partner. The partner may use the book to see if everything important has been covered.

Social Studies/Science
Use with short text selections. Have students alternate sections throughout a chapter. The partner can prompt for additional information.

Assessment

Use teacher observation during paired retellings, discussion, and a quiz or test to determine comprehension. Teacher observation should include monitoring the involvement of individual students during the paired retelling. Discussion helps determine students' comprehension level by assessing their responses after reading. Encourage responses from students who appear off task. Students should correctly respond to 80% of the questions during a discussion or quiz. If students do not respond correctly, have their partners assist them and refer back to the text.

Gunning, 1996

Fostering Cooperative Learning

Circle-Seat-Center

This strategy allows students to work in small peer groups and go over all the information the teacher would like to cover. The strategy is an excellent way to reinforce information in a variety of ways: The Circle group focuses on verbal learning, the Seat group focuses on visual learning, and the Center group focuses on tactile learning. This also allows students who learn through different modalities the opportunity to learn through their strength.

Procedure

First, instruct students to read the text. Following this, divide the class into three groups based on instructional needs. Give each group an assignment: Circle, Seat, or Center. The Circle group covers information in the text with your assistance. The Seat group members work individually or within their group to go over the text information using worksheets and study sheets. The Center group works on projects, individually or in the group, related to the information covered in the text. After a designated amount of time, students rotate to another group.

Language Arts
Topic: Parts of Speech
Circle: Discuss and clarify the topic for students.
Seat: Students work on identifying the parts of speech using worksheets or skills sheets.
Center: Students create cards to be used in a game.

Social Studies
Topic: Fall of Rome
Circle: Discuss text, including reasons for the fall of Rome.
Seat: Respond to questions and do worksheets.
Center: Create a timeline of the Roman Empire.

Science
Topic: Matter in Solution
Circle: Discuss the types of solutions.
Seat: Complete worksheets or respond to questions at end of section.
Center: Create charts to classify types of solutions.

Assessment

Use teacher observation of information covered during discussion, correct answers on worksheets, and evaluation of information covered in projects to determine students' level of comprehension.

Ivey, 1999b

Classwide Peer Tutoring (CWP)

This strategy enables students to learn from their peers and requires 30 to 45 minutes of class time. This strategy is helpful because it allows students to express understanding of the text in a nonthreatening manner with their peers.

Procedure

First, pair students. (This pairing should change each time this strategy is used.) During the first 10 minutes, one student (tutor) assists the other student (tutee) with content information from a specific unit or subject area, presented orally and/or visually. For the next 5 to 10 minutes, the tutor assesses the tutee's learning by having the tutee restate the information orally and in writing. The tutor gives two points to the tutee for each correct piece of information. If the tutor has to assist the tutee, the tutee gets one point when the information is given correctly. The object is to go over as much information as possible and gain as many points as possible. Next, the pair should switch roles and repeat the process. At the end of class, check the points scored for each individual.

The students may need to practice this strategy a few times before they are comfortable with it. As they become familiar with the strategy, the level of success should increase.

Language Arts
Discuss concepts in grammar and usage, rules, vocabulary, and information in a story.

Social Studies
Discuss various topics related to life in Ancient Greece, such as "in the marketplace," "at home," "slavery," and "women." Have specific information you would like the student to know pertaining to each topic.

Science
Discuss structure, functions, and parts of a plant; life cycle of a moss; structure/function of a flower; methods of seed dispersal; and role of stomata in gas exchange. Compare/contrast vascular and nonvascular, plants that produce seeds in cones and those in plants, photosynthesis and respiration.

Math
Go over concepts such as ratio, proportion, percent, area, volume, and equations.

Arreaga-Mayer, 1998; Delquadri, Greenwood, Stretton, & Hall, 1983

(continued)

Assessment

Use evaluation of points earned, discussion, teacher questioning, and a quiz or test to determine comprehension. A worksheet can be created with specific information to be covered and specific points assigned to assist the tutor. Monitor the involvement of individual students and their responses. Discussion can be used to determine students' level of comprehension by assessing their responses after reading. Encourage responses from students who appear off task. Students should correctly respond to 80% of the questions in a discussion, on a quiz, or on a worksheet. Allow students who do not respond correctly to spend additional time working with their partner in going over the information.

Group Investigation

This strategy allows each student to be personally responsible for a small portion of the information that is covered. Although students only study and present their information, they must listen and pay attention to the information presented by all other students. This is effective because students tend to like to listen to their peers. This strategy is a powerful way to quickly cover a large amount of information.

Procedure

Students work in groups of two to six members. Discuss the main topic that is being covered in class. Each group then selects a subtopic related to the main topic, and each group member researches a portion of that topic. Students share their information within their group to assure they have covered their individual topic well. Each group then presents its information to the entire class.

Language Arts
Main Topic: Parts of Speech
Subtopics: noun, pronoun, adjective, adverb, preposition

Social Studies
Main Topic: Earth's Physical Geography
Subtopics: land, air, water, climate, weather

Science
Main Topic: States of Matter
Subtopics: solids, liquids, gases

Assessment

Determine if complete and correct information was given in the class presentations. A written assessment also may be used.

Hendrix, 1999

Jigsaw

Jigsaw allows students to work with their peers and to learn information from one another. This strategy allows for all members of the class to receive information about an entire section in a text. It is a collaborative strategy that ensures the participation of all students.

Procedure

First, group three to six students in teams. Give each team member a topic on which to become an "expert." The teams then split up and find the students from the other teams who are working on their topic. After working in the topic groups, students return to their teams and present the information they gained.

Language Arts
When reviewing a specific story, assign team members with a component such as character, plot, setting, problem, or resolution.

Social Studies
When studying the five themes of geography, assign each member of a team one of the topics: location, place, human-environment interaction, movement, and regions.

Science
Give each member of a group a topic such as acids, bases, and salts.

Math
Use as review. After studying fractions, divide into groups and assign each member a topic such as adding, subtracting, dividing, and multiplying.

Assessment

Determine students' level of comprehension by the correct number of responses in a quiz or through discussion of information presented by each team.

Aronson, 1997; Hendrix, 1999

Learning Together

For this strategy, students work in groups of four or five members on a single worksheet that covers information that has either been instructed or is in the text. Everyone contributes and must know the information. At the end of the activity, the group submits a single worksheet.

Students tend to feel more comfortable when they are able to work with others. This may lessen their anxiety and help them to learn more. The group sheet is a quick evaluation for student comprehension, but follow-up for individual accountability is necessary.

Procedure

Group students in small groups of four to five members. Have them work together on a worksheet that covers information that has either been instructed or is in the text. Everyone contributes and must know the information. At the end of the activity, the group submits a single sheet.

Language Arts
Use this activity with parts of speech and grammar rules.

Social Studies/Science
Complete a worksheet or questions from the end of a chapter, or create your own worksheets to cover the information discussed.

Math
Students work on sheets that cover addition, subtraction, multiplication, and division of fractions.

Assessment

Determine students' comprehension by evaluating the group worksheet and giving individual quizzes.

Hendrix, 1999

Partner Prediction

This strategy gives students the opportunity to work with their peers and make predictions about a story or section. Because students are sharing their ideas with a partner, more students will be able to discuss prediction and they will not feel self-conscious about speaking in front of the entire class. If a student is having difficulties with prediction, partner him or her with someone who is able to do it, and he or she will have the opportunity to see how the process is done.

Procedure

First, identify places in the text to stop and predict what might happen next. Then read the title and first portion aloud and ask what students think the story will be about. Students should be seated next to partners so they can share their ideas with each other. This process is repeated throughout the reading. When the end of the selection is near, stop and ask how students think it will end.

Language Arts
Topic: "Cats on the Run"
Students discuss what this story may be about. As reading begins, students learn it is about tigers in the wild. Students discuss what might happen in the story.

Social Studies
Topic: Japan
Students discuss what they know. Mention origami, and ask students to discuss what they have learned to make or what they would like to learn. Reading covers haiku and the Japanese language.

Science
Topic: Plants
Students discuss what they know. Reading covers types of trees and flowers. Students discuss how to tell the difference and which ones they have seen, and they discuss what else might be covered in the text.

Assessment

Through teacher observation and discussion, determine accuracy of student predictions. Monitor the involvement of individual students during the paired retelling. Discussion can be used to determine students' level of comprehension by assessing their responses after reading. Encourage responses from students who appear off task. Students should correctly respond to 80% of the questions during a discussion. Change partners to increase accuracy if necessary.

Buehl, 1997

Reciprocal Teaching

This strategy allows students to begin to work together and to "teach" each other as they take over the discussion.

Procedure

Begin by dividing the class into small groups. Each group should then read and discuss a short section from the text. After all the groups have completed this, bring the entire class together and discuss the information that was covered. Start by leading the discussion, then gradually decrease your input and allow student input to increase. Encourage the participation of all students.

Language Arts
Topic: Short Section of a Story
Ask the following questions: Why did the main character react as he or she did? What is the importance of the setting in this story?

Social Studies
Topic: Earth's Human Geography
Ask the following questions: Where do people live? Why do they migrate? What problems will the growing population cause?

Science
Go over types of matter, or ask, What is an ecosystem?

Assessment

Use discussion, quizzes, and observation to determine if material is understood. Observation should include monitoring the involvement of individual students and their responses. Discussion can be used to determine students' levels of comprehension by assessing their responses after reading. Encourage responses from students who appear off task. Students should correctly respond to 80% of the questions during a discussion or given on a quiz. Encourage students to assist one another.

Language Arts

Social Studies

Science

Math

Aarnoutse & Brand-Gruwel, 1997; Banikowski & Mehring, 1999; Palincsar, 1984

Silent With Support

This strategy simply involves allowing the students to read the text silently while sitting with partners or in small groups. As they read silently, the students may get help from those around them if needed.

This can be used in any subject area. It is important to group the students according to mixed ability.

Procedure

Group students as partners or in small groups. Allow them to read the story or text selection silently while sitting with their partner or group. Explain that they may consult with their group if they have questions or need assistance during the reading.

Language Arts
Use the activity with stories, poems, or grammar lessons. Students can ask about vocabulary, concepts, or directions.

Social Studies/Science
Use with any selection of text. Students may get assistance with vocabulary, concepts, or directions.

Math
Use with word problems.

Assessment

Determine comprehension through discussion, quizzes/tests, or teacher questioning. Discussion and teacher questioning can be used to determine students' level of comprehension by assessing their responses after reading. Encourage responses from students who appear off task. Students should correctly respond to 80% of the questions during a discussion or given on a quiz. If students are unable to respond correctly, you may want to regroup certain students to improve the "support" given by the partners.

Lamme & Beckett, 1992

Skit Performance

This strategy allows students to be involved in their learning. It provides cooperative learning because each student has a part to play in the story or contributes to the script writing. Through their participation students are able to demonstrate their understanding of the concepts covered.

Procedure

Students read a story or text, then write and perform a skit or play about the concepts they have studied. This does not need to be a major production. It is just a way to determine if they understand what they read.

Language Arts
After studying a story, have students pretend to be characters from the story and give a general idea of the story or perform a scene.

Social Studies
After studying several cultures, have students pretend to be people from these cultures meeting for the first time, discussing similarities and differences.

Assessment

Determine comprehension through discussion and correct display of concepts. Discussion can be used to determine students' comprehension by assessing their responses after reading. Students should be able to communicate the main concepts in the text through their skit performance. If they are unable to do so, use discussion to reinforce the main concepts with the students and allow them to alter their skit to include the main concepts. Quizzes or tests may also be used to assess understanding following the performance.

Cochran, 1993

Student Teams—Achievement Division (STAD)

This strategy is useful in reviewing information from a lesson and is most effective when the questions have a single correct answer. Students are able to work together cooperatively.

Procedure

After teaching a lesson, group students into four-member, mixed-ability teams. Each team works together to make certain that every member of the group has mastered the information. Use a quiz to go over the information, and give an individual and team score.

The steps for this process are as follows:

- Teach concept/skill—check understanding
- Team study—rank students and group as follows: one high achiever, two average achievers, and one low achiever; teams complete worksheets and are responsible for all members mastering the concept
- Test—check individual understanding; give team points based on improvement over previous average: 10 below average or more = 0 points; 10 below to 1 below average = 10 points; 0 to 10 above average = 20 points; more than 10 above average = 30 points
- Team recognition for team with highest score

Giving team scores in addition to individual scores motivates the teams to make certain everyone understands the information that has been covered.

Language Arts
The strategy is best for information such as grammar or punctuation; students should go over the rules and correct usage.

Social Studies
Review and discuss the five themes of geography; students should be able to identify the five themes and characteristics of each.

Science
Using topics such as acids, bases, and salts, students should be able to identify properties of each and know how to determine where a substance belongs.

Math
The strategy works well with simple equations and problems; students may use flashcards or cover more difficult work using paper to solve the problems.

Hendrix, 1999; Nesbit & Rogers, 1997; Slavin, 1988

Assessment

Use discussion, quizzes, and tests to ascertain level of understanding. Discussion can be used to determine students' level of comprehension by assessing their responses after reading. Encourage responses from students who appear off task. Students should correctly respond to 80% of the questions during a discussion or given on a quiz or test.

Teams-Games-Tournament (TGT)

Competition in the classroom can be motivational. Students work in teams, which promotes cooperative learning. Due to their competitive nature, students will tend to cooperate with members of their team in order to prevail over the other teams.

Procedure

To use this strategy, group students homogeneously by past performance into groups of three or four students. At the end of each week, hold a tournament based on the information that was covered during the week. Hold tournaments between teams of matched ability. Recognize the winning teams.

There is flexibility in organizing these tournaments. Change groups as necessary; however, it is important that the groups be equally matched. A study period prior to the tournament allows students to go over the important information that was covered.

Language Arts
Topic: Vocabulary
Go over words/definitions, use synonyms, and fill in the blanks in sentences.

Social Studies
Topic: Immigrants to the United States
Discuss catastrophes in the 1880s, reasons immigrants came, and problems they encountered in the United States.

Science
Topic: States of Matter
Discuss solids, liquids, gases, properties, and matter.

Math
Topic: Geometry
Study shapes, area, volume, measurement, and formulas.

Assessment

Determine understanding through correct student responses in the tournament.

Hendrix, 1999

Think-Pair-Share/Think-Pair-Square

This is a partner or group activity that allows students to work together to check for comprehension.

Procedure

After reading a story or section of text, students should think of things they already know, decide what the reading reminds them of, and determine what might happen next. Students then "Pair and Share" (two students) or "Pair and Square" (four students) and discuss the things they have thought about.

Language Arts
After covering a short story or selection, discuss character, plot, motivation, setting, and resolution.

Social Studies
After covering South America, discuss people, culture, religion, land, climate, and resources.

Science
After covering animal habitats, discuss what animals need to survive and how different animals adapt.

Math
After reading a word problem, determine what is being asked, what information is given, and what mathematical function or formula is needed to solve the problem.

Assessment

Use discussion, quizzes, or tests during or following the activity. Discussion can be used to determine students' level of comprehension by assessing their responses after reading. Encourage responses from students who appear off task. Students should correctly respond to 80% of the questions during a discussion or given on a quiz or test.

Banikowski & Mehring, 1999; Bromley & Modlo, 1997

Writing Word Problems

This strategy is useful in improving comprehension of word problems. Encouraging students to bring their cultures and background knowledge into the word problems helps them to become active participants in the learning process.

Procedure

Have students work in cooperative groups and create their own word problems that incorporate the concepts they have been studying. Assign roles in the groups if needed. Monitor the groups and let them know that each individual is accountable. As students are creating their problems, give feedback, making certain the problems are clear.

Math

After studying a section and dealing with word problems, have the students create word problems using students their own age and circumstances with which they are familiar (movies, going out to eat, school).

Assessment

Have students from one group read their problem aloud while students from another group work the problem on the board. This will help in determining if the problem is clear and contains all the necessary information. Evaluate the group that is presenting the problem as well as the group attempting to solve the problem.

Muth, 1997; Winograd & Higgins, 1995

Connecting to Previous Knowledge

Activate Prior Knowledge

This strategy is designed to determine what students already know about the topic that is going to be studied. This will help to create interest prior to reading.

Activating prior knowledge allows students to feel that they are somehow connected to the topic being studied, helping to create a more positive learning environment and helping students feel that they are a part of the learning process.

Procedure

Before beginning a text, discuss the topic that will be covered. Have the students share what they already know about the topic. Find ways to relate the knowledge they have with the material that needs to be covered.

Language Arts
Topic: Story About Snakes
Ask students, What do you know about snakes? How can you tell if they are poisonous? What snakes are common in our area?

Social Studies
Topic: Climate
Ask students, How does climate affect vegetation? What kinds of plants only grow in certain areas?

Science
Topic: Tornadoes
Ask students, What do you know about tornadoes? What do you know about thunderstorms? Are they similar? What would you do if you were caught in a tornado?

Math
Topic: Multiplication With Decimals
Ask students, When are decimals used in everyday life (e.g., money)? If you were purchasing several items at the same price, how could you quickly figure out the total cost?

Assessment

Discuss each question and determine from students' answers which students need additional information before beginning a lesson. As the lesson progresses, continue discussion and questions to determine students' comprehension of the topic.

Bean & Zigmond, 1994; Pearson & Johnson, 1978; Vacca & Vacca, 1989

Anticipation Guide

This strategy allows students to consider thoughts and opinions they have about various topics in order to create an interest in the material that is being covered and to establish a purpose for reading the material.

This strategy works best with topics such as literature, science, and social studies that require information in order to develop opinions. Although subjects such as grammar and mathematics are more skill related, there are instances in which an Anticipation Guide with modifications would be useful.

Procedure

Begin by listing three or more debatable statements about a topic that students are going to study. Ask the students to identify whether they agree or disagree with the statements. Explain that the students need to read the text carefully and see if they can find statements that support their own views. After they read the text, discuss the original statements to see if the students maintain their original view or if they have changed their opinion.

When constructing an Anticipation Guide, keep the following in mind:

- Analyze the material and determine main ideas.
- Write the ideas in short, declarative statements. Avoid abstractions.
- Put the statements in a format that will encourage anticipation and predictions.
- Discuss readers' predictions and anticipations before reading.
- Assign the text. Have students evaluate the statements according to the author's intent and purpose.
- Contrast the predictions with the author's intended meaning.

Language Arts

Social Studies

Science

Math

Language Arts
Topic: Writing a persuasive paper
Statements: Students should wear uniforms in school.
              Students should be allowed to choose whatever classes they want to take.
              There should be no dress code in schools.

Banikowski & Mehring, 1999; Gunning, 1996; Herber, 1978; Vacca & Vacca, 1989

(continued)

Social Studies

Topic: Ancient Mediterranean civilization

Statements: Living in the ancient Mediterranean civilization was rewarding for all people.
Ancient writing is similar to our writing of today.
There were no schools in ancient civilizations.

Science

Topic: Plant life

Statements: All types of plants can be grown anywhere.
Poisonous plants are easy to identify.
All plants come from seeds.

Assessment

After discussing each statement, listening to student responses, and reading the text, go over the statements again to see if students are able to support their response to the statements.

Brainstorming

This strategy allows students to share their knowledge and experiences related to a topic, creating interest in the text. The strategy facilitates comprehension by activating prior knowledge; however, it is more structured than the Activating Prior Knowledge strategy.

Brainstorming is most effective when a topic is given and students state things they think of related to the topic. A limited amount of time should be given for this activity before continuing with a discussion.

Procedure

Begin by listing words or concepts that will be in the text. Then ask students to identify what they already know about these—in writing or orally. This can be done individually, in small groups, or in a large group. Share all the information with the entire class before reading the text. Add information to help students better understand the concepts.

Language Arts
Before reading a story about fantastic creatures, brainstorm the following:
 what is fantasy
 creatures
 fantasy creatures (e.g., the
  Loch Ness Monster)

Social Studies
Before reading about Egypt, brainstorm the following:
 pyramids
 mummies
 workers
 pharaohs

Science
Before reading about types of solutions, brainstorm the following:
 colloids and suspensions
 concentrates
 saturation

Assessment

After reading the text, review the words or concepts that were covered originally. Then ask students to identify new information they learned that was not listed in the Brainstorming activity.

Banikowski & Mehring, 1999; Cochran, 1993; Vacca & Vacca, 1989

Directed Reading Activity (DRA)

Often students are instructed to read without being told why the information is important or what they are expected to learn. DRA provides students with a purpose for reading using the sharing of previous knowledge to build understanding.

Procedure

The components of this activity are as follows:

- Before reading (Prereading)—Establish purpose, build background, and motivate.
- During reading (Reader-Text Interactions)—Prompt active response for reading.
- After reading (Postreading)—Reinforce and extend ideas.

First, go over key concepts and vocabulary words. Next, tell students why the information is needed (e.g., for a test, quiz, grade, demonstration) and what information you would like them to acquire. Then allow the students to read silently.

Finally, have a follow-up activity such as a demonstration, speech, questions, or quiz. The follow-up activity can be extended by linking it to other activities or assignments.

Language Arts
- Tell students they will explore different types of poems before they are asked to write a poem of their own.
- Go over related vocabulary.
- Have students read the selection independently.
- Have students volunteer to read aloud with expression.
- Give assignment to write poem.

Social Studies
- Pose this question to students: If history repeats itself, will what happened to the Roman Empire possibly happen to the United States?
- Go over vocabulary.
- Give a test or quiz.
- Give students sections of text and have them make posters to discuss.
- Link to politics.

Science
- Have students think of impressive views of landscapes they have seen, and explain that you will cover various types of landscapes.
- Go over vocabulary such as *landforms*, *constellations*, *contour lines*, *elevation*, *latitude*, *longitude*.
- Link to geography and social studies.

Math
- Tell students the information they will be learning will be used throughout their lives, especially when purchasing items and balancing a checkbook.
- Go over integers and the concept of negative and positive.
- Explain that they will be working in pairs to try to balance an imaginary checkbook.

Cochran, 1993; Gunning, 1996; Vacca & Vacca, 1989

Assessment

Through the follow-up activity, questions, and discussion, determine students' comprehension of the given topic. The follow-up activity and discussion can be used to determine students' level of comprehension by assessing their responses. Encourage responses from students who appear off task. Students should correctly respond to 80% of the questions during a discussion or given on a quiz or test. If students do not respond correctly, provide additional instruction and information. Students may be allowed to work together if necessary.

FLIP

This strategy is used prior to reading in order to determine the friendliness, language, interest, and prior knowledge regarding a reading selection. Once the students have discussed their prior knowledge about the selection, they may feel more interested in the topic and will be able to contribute to a discussion.

Procedure

The steps for this strategy are as follows:

[F]riendliness—Determine what features are easy to understand (friendly) and difficult to understand (unfriendly).

[L]anguage—Determine what terms the students might need to learn more about.

[I]nterest—Determine the level of interest, which may affect the level of involvement.

[P]rior Knowledge—Determine what the students already know about what is being asked.

Discuss each of these areas with the students and determine ways to improve the areas that might cause difficulty. For example, if the features make reading difficult, discuss headings, paragraphs, and layout to decide how to make it friendlier. Occasionally it will be evident that some of the terms need to be discussed prior to reading. If the level of interest is not high, find ways to relate some part of the selection to the students to give them more motivation to read.

Language Arts
Topic: *Maniac Magee* by Jerry Spinelli
F—The story has a fairly easy reading level.
L—Locate words such as *maniac*.
I—Discuss what it would be like to grow up on your own.
P—Ask students if they know children like Maniac Magee.

Social Studies
Topic: Early African Civilizations
F—The text is divided into sections.
L—Introduce words such as *civilization*.
I—Discuss how early civilizations affect present-day society.
P—Discuss what students already know about African civilizations.

Science
Topic: Nature of Light
F—The text is divided into sections with questions.
L—Go over words such as *opaque, translucent,* and *transparent*.
I—Think how fast light moves.
P—Ask what students already know about light.

Math
Topic: Decimals
F—Words are easy to understand.
L—Students need to recognize decimals and what they mean.
I—Show interest when related to money.
P—Discuss use of decimals in money.

Fuentes, 1998

Assessment

After the FLIP strategy, determine if additional language needs to be introduced and if more interest should be developed. Discussion and questions can be used to determine students' level of comprehension by assessing their responses after reading. Teachers should encourage responses from students who appear off task. Students should correctly respond to 80% of the questions in a discussion or on a quiz or test. Review specific steps in FLIP for students who do not give correct answers.

Nonfiction Trade Books

After introducing a selected topic, use nonfiction trade books to help students expand their knowledge on that particular topic. Reading material that is appropriate for their individual reading levels helps students to be successful readers by decreasing the frustration that might exist with material that is too advanced. Also, relating this reading material to information that was previously covered enables students to make a connection with this knowledge.

Procedure

Begin by locating trade books that relate to the class topic, and make these available to the students. These books may help students to relate to the topic and learn information that they might be able to share with the class. It is important to be aware of the reading level of each trade book; do not choose levels that would be too challenging for the student because this will only discourage them.

Social Studies
Read trade books about different cultures, languages, and religions.

Science
Read books about earthquakes, volcanoes, moving water, plants, and animals.

Assessment

Through discussion, quizzes, and individual reports, assess students' knowledge regarding the topic. Discussion can be used to determine students' level of comprehension by assessing their responses after reading. Encourage responses from students who appear off task. Students should correctly respond to 80% of the questions during a discussion or given on a quiz. Individual reports can also assist the teacher in assessing students' level of comprehension.

Manning, 1999a

Prediction Log

This strategy acts as a motivator and gives purpose to the reading. It also allows the students to be totally honest in their prediction and to do a self-evaluation. Based on what students have learned in previous years, they are able to make predictions.

Procedure

The first step in this strategy is to ask a question related to the topic that the students are going to study. For example, What was daily life like in Ancient Egypt? Next, have students write their predictions in a log. After reading the text, have students write in their logs what the answer is and if they were correct in their prediction.

Collect the logs periodically to see if there are students who are having difficulties with this skill.

Language Arts
After reading about people from different backgrounds, ask, What would it be like to visit someone nearby who lives in a totally different way than you? What might he or she be like?

Social Studies
What was daily life like in Ancient Egypt?

Science
What particles can be carried by wind?
How do sand dunes move?
What types of damage can be caused by the wind?

Assessment

Comprehension is determined through teacher evaluation of a logical prediction. This must be done on an individual basis using students' logs.

Ivey, 1999a; Vacca & Vacca, 1989

ReQuest

This strategy encourages students to build on previous knowledge and think about what might be important information in the assigned reading. It also gives them the opportunity to write questions about things they do not understand. One of the advantages to this strategy is that it breaks the text into short sections so it will not appear overwhelming to students.

Procedure

The first step is to choose the text to be covered. Make sure students are familiar with the entire selection. Next, have the students read the first paragraph or short section and have them think of questions to ask about the topic as they read. After the reading, have students ask their questions and use the text to answer. Next, ask higher level questions you have prepared. Continue reading the entire selection and have a question-answer session at the end of each section.

Language Arts
Read the introduction to a story. Have students ask questions about the characters, setting, and plot. Continue reading short sections. Prepare questions such as, Do you think the characters are acting in the way they should? Why or why not? What would you have done in this situation? What is one thing that could have changed the entire outcome of this story?

Social Studies
Read the beginning of a chapter on the Fertile Crescent. Ask why it was called this. What is known about this area from long ago? End with questions such as, What do you think caused this culture to last throughout time?

Science
When discussing a topic such as sound waves, ask students how they think Helen Keller learned to speak or how Beethoven was able to compose music even after he became deaf.

Assessment

Discuss and evaluate teachers' and students' questions and answers. Discussion can be used to determine students' level of comprehension by assessing their responses after reading. Encourage responses from students who appear off task. Students should correctly respond to 80% of the questions during a discussion.

Gunning, 1996; Manzo, 1969; Vacca & Vacca, 1989

Story Content Instruction

This strategy uses students' existing knowledge as a framework for introducing the story, helping students relate more to the story and feel that they can contribute to the discussion.

Procedure

Prior to reading, give intensive instruction about potentially difficult parts of the story or text. Relate each part to things the students already know. After completing this, have students read the story or text and discuss.

Language Arts
Topic: A Family
Discuss what students consider a family. Have them describe their families.

Social Studies
Topic: Hindu religion in India
Discuss the importance of religion and various religions; describe religions students are familiar with in their community.

Science
Topic: Metamorphosis
Discuss the various cartoons and videos dealing with characters that "morph" (e.g., Animorphs).

Assessment

Through discussion of the topic, determine what knowledge students have regarding the topic.

Dole, Brown, & Woodrow, 1996

Improving Organization

Character Perspective Charting (CPC)

This strategy gives students a visual organizer that shows the relationship between a character's perspective and the events in a story. Adding characters' perspectives can clarify why they reacted in certain ways in the story, which gives more depth to the characters.

Procedure

After the students have read the entire story, they should use a map or chart to list the important events (problems, resolution, etc.). Assign each student one character. Students discuss the characters' perspectives during each of the events in the story on the map or chart. Ask questions to focus on the characters' motives and reactions.

Language Arts
Character:_____

Perspective
Thoughts/feelings:_____

Motivation:_____

Events
Problem: _____

Resolution: _____

Outcome:_____

Social Studies
Character: Abraham Lincoln

Perspective
Thoughts/feelings:_____

Motivation:_____

Events
Problem: _____

Resolution: _____

Outcome:_____

Assessment

Through discussion and evaluation of the completed maps or charts, determine if students correctly identify the motives and reactions of characters.

Emery, 1996; Shanahan & Shanahan, 1997

Expectation Outline

This is an excellent organizational strategy that can be a useful study guide and will assist with comprehension. As students become more comfortable with the outline format, they may be able to create their own outlines for a variety of subjects and topics.

Procedure

First, create an outline, leaving several blanks for the students to use when covering information from the text. Have students fill in the blanks with the appropriate information as they come to it. (Filling in some of the blanks for the students allows those who may have difficulties to check their understanding of what is being asked.)

Language Arts

Topic: Short Story "Your Three Minutes Are Up"

I. Recall
    A. Libby wanted _____
    B. Her parents decided to _____
II. Interpreting _____
    A. Her parents _____ fair because _____
    B. Libby's friends were mad because _____
III. Evaluating
    A. Other alternatives that might have been used _____
    B. Lesson from the story _____

Social Studies

Topic: East Asia's Physical Geography

I. Land and water
    A. Physical features
    B. _____
II. Climate and _____
    A. Weather _____ - _____
    B. Storms _____ - _____
III. _____
    A. Minerals _____
    B. Forests _____

(continued)

Vacca & Vacca, 1989

Science

Topic: States of Matter

I. Solid - _____

    A. Characteristics

        1. _____

        2. _____

    B. Examples

        1. ice

        2. _____

II. _____ - _____

    A. Characteristics

        1. _____

        2. _____

    B. Examples

        1. water

        2. _____

III. _____ - _____

    A. Characteristics

        1. _____

        2. _____

    B. Examples

        1. steam

        2. _____

Assessment

Determine if students have correctly covered the information by evaluating the completed outline and discussing the information. Discussion can be used to determine students' level of comprehension by assessing their responses after reading. Students should correctly respond to 80% of the questions during a discussion or given in their outline.

K-W-L (Know-Want to Know-Learned)

K-W-L gives students a purpose for reading and gives them an active role before, during, and after reading. This strategy helps them to think about the information they already know and to celebrate the learning of new information. It also strengthens their ability to develop questions in a variety of topics and to assess their own learning.

Procedure

Before reading, ask students to brainstorm what is known about a topic. They should categorize what is prior knowledge, predict or anticipate what the text might be about, and create questions to be answered. During reading, have the students refer to their questions and think of what might answer them. After reading, have the class discuss the information, write responses to their questions, and organize the information.

This strategy may be done on a sheet with three columns: Know, Want to Know, Learned. Guide the instruction the first few times it is used. Modeling is effective for the initial use.

Language Arts

Know	Want to Know	Learned
nouns	adverbs	modifies a verb, adjective, or another adverb
pronouns	prepositions	combines with noun, pronoun, or noun equivalent
verbs	proper punctuation	correct use of commas, colons, semicolons, quotation marks
adjectives		
capitalization		

Social Studies

Topic: Ancient Egypt

Know	Want to Know	Learned
pharaohs	Why did they mummify people?	believed in an afterlife
buried dead		
pyramid	How long did it take to build a pyramid?	sometimes a lifetime
mummified people		

Banikowski & Mehring, 1999; Gunning, 1996; Jeffrey, 1997; Ogle, 1986, 1994; Warren & Flynt, 1995

(continued)

Science
Topic: Earthquakes

Know	*Want to Know*	*Learned*
shaking near coast a lot lately	What causes them?	shifting of rock
	Can you prevent them?	no, but you can build buildings to withstand it

Math
Topic: Adding Fractions

Know	*Want to Know*	*Learned*
adding with like denominators	adding with different denominators	find a common denominator, change fraction, then add
changing improper fractions to mixed fractions		

Assessment

Through comparison of the "Want to Know" with the "Learned" column, class discussion, and a quiz or test, determine if students have learned the information they originally wanted to know more about. If there are still items they want to learn additional information about, discuss this with them. Ideally, each student should complete the "Learned" column with completed information about items in the "Want to Know" column along with new information they learned along the way.

Mapping

Mapping provides a visual guide for students to clarify textual information such as characters, setting, problems, reactions, and outcome. This strategy allows you to visually determine students' comprehension, and it provides students with a strategy that they can use on their own when they are dealing with other topics.

Procedure

Model an example of a map for students, talking through each step and having students assist in filling in the different areas. After comprehension of this strategy is assured, have students complete various maps on their own.

Language Arts

Social Studies

Science

Math

Language Arts
Characters: _____
Setting: Place_____ Time _____
Problem: _____
Events: _____
_____
_____
_____

Resolution: _____
Outcome: _____

Social Studies
Topic: Ancient Egypt

pharaohs	medicines	pyramids	afterlife	gods	mummification
___	___	___	___	___	___
___	___	___	___	___	___
___	___	___	___	___	___
___	___	___	___	___	___

Science
Topic: States of Matter
Solids: _____
Liquids: _____
Gases: _____

Assessment

Evaluate students' maps to determine level of comprehension by the percentage of correct responses.

Swanson & De Le Paz, 1998; Vacca & Vacca, 1989; Vallecorsa & deBettencourt, 1997

ORDER

This strategy can be used for a variety of subject areas to assist students in visually organizing and reviewing information. Once the strategy is learned, students can use it independently.

Procedure

First instruct the class on the following steps in the strategy and assist them until they become familiar enough to use it on their own:

[O]pen your mind and take notes.

[R]ecognize the structure of the text.

[D]raw an organizer—something visual (e.g., outline, map, chart).

[E]xplain the organizer to others.

[R]euse it as a study guide.

It is helpful to model this strategy several times and then have students assist in completing a visual organizer before they are required to do this on their own.

Language Arts
Parts of Speech Organizer

Article	Adjective	Noun	Adverb	Verb	Prepositional Phrase

Social Studies

Weather	*Climate*
day-to-day changes in the air temperature precipitation	average weather over many years

Science
States of Matter

Solids	
Liquids	
Gases	

Math
Converting Fractions to Decimals
1. Set up numerator divided by denominator.
2. Place decimal and add zero if needed.
3. Divide up to three places past the decimal.
4. Round to the nearest hundredth.

Bulgren & Scanlon, 1998

Assessment

Assess students' explanations of their organizers and evaluate the information included in the organizer to determine comprehension.

Language Arts

Social Studies

Science

Math

PLAN

This is a graphic organizer in which students create a map to visually organize and better understand the information that has been covered.

Procedure

There are four steps in this process:

[P]redict the content/structure by using chapter titles and subheadings.

[L]ocate known and unknown information. Students can indicate this by placing a ✓ by things they know and a ? by things they do not know.

[A]dd words or phrases to the ? as students locate information about the topic.

[N]ote new understanding of information and use it in instruction.

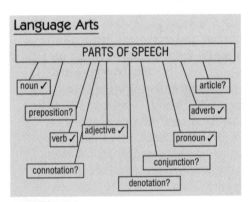

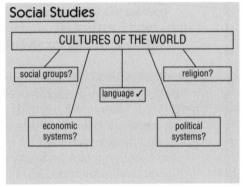

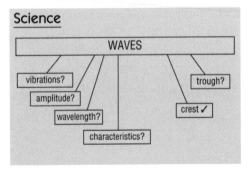

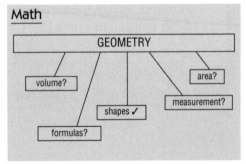

Assessment

Evaluate the answers that individual students provide to the questions in their organizer.

Caverly, Mandeville, & Nicholson, 1995; Vacca & Vacca, 1989

Promoting Independent Learning

CONCEPT

This strategy clarifies and enhances information related to a single concept. The strategy is involved, but it is beneficial when the teacher is beginning to teach a unit or concept that might be challenging for the students. It allows students to use the format provided to move ahead independently with their learning.

Procedure

This strategy involves the following steps:

[C]onvey the concept to the students by naming the topic that is being studied.

[O]ffer the overall concept by explaining what it is related to.

[N]ote the key words involved with the concept.

[C]lassify characteristics about the topic.

[E]xplore some examples and see if they fit the key concept definition.

[P]ractice with new examples. (Give examples and assist the students to see if the new examples fit the key concept definition.)

[T]ie down a definition.

Language Arts
Topic: Haiku
C—haiku
O—a Japanese poem
N—syllables
C—3 lines, 5-7-5 syllables
E—sunlight on the lake
    glittering, shimmering bright
    sparkles like the stars
P—Write various examples.
T—A haiku is a three-line Japanese form of poetry that (in general English form) is no more than 17 syllables and is usually in the 5-7-5 format.

Social Studies
Topic: Settlers
C—Settlers
O—people in America
N—move, new (use prior knowledge and text)
C—Settlers move to an unfamiliar land, build permanent houses, bring their personal values.
E—Pioneers in 1800s American West? (yes) Native Americans in 1800s American West? (no)
P—Give examples of groups; students indicate if they meet the requirements of settlers.
T—For our purposes, settlers are people in America who have moved to an unfamiliar place, built permanent houses, and brought their own values to their new home.

Assessment

By discussing and checking the "P" (practice) and "T" (tying down a definition), determine if students clearly understand the concept.

Bulgren & Scanlon, 1998

DISSECT Word Identification Strategy

This strategy offers students several means to learn unfamiliar words.

Procedure

There are seven steps in this process; however, once the students understand the meaning of the word, it is not necessary to continue through the remaining steps:

[D]iscover the word's context by using clues in the text.

[I]solate the prefix and assess the meaning (skip if there is no prefix).

[S]eparate the suffix (skip if there is no suffix).

[S]ay the stem by reading the root.

[E]xamine the stem by separating letters to make decoding easier.

[C]heck with someone if necessary.

[T]ry the dictionary if still having difficulties.

Language Arts
Word: *incomprehensible*
The steps would lead to the word *comprehend*. The definition of *understand* would be used. Finally, the definition "unable to understand" would be given for the original word.

Social Studies
Word: *inalienable*
The steps would lead to the word *alien*. The definition "belonging to another person" would be used. Finally, the definition "unable to transfer to another" would be given for the original word.

Science
Word: *unsaturated*
The steps would lead to the word *saturated*, then *saturate*. The definition "full of moisture" would be used. Finally, the definition "capable of absorbing" would be given for the original word.

Math
Word: *inequality*
The steps would lead to the word *equal*. The definition "identical in mathematical value" would be used. Finally, the definition "not the same value" would be given for the original word.

Assessment

Through teacher questioning and discussion, determine if students are able to understand the meaning of the word and use it in context. Answering aloud regarding the word's definition can assist in this. Allow students to contribute their suggestions to the correct meaning of a word with guidance from the teacher. If necessary, refer students back to one of the steps in the DISSECT strategy.

Bryant, Ugel, Thompson, & Hamff, 1999

Narrow and Enlarge the Text

This strategy is designed to help individual students by simplifying the amount of information that is covered. Although this strategy is not for everyone, it is helpful to the individual student whose reading level may be below grade level and who looks at text as overwhelming and difficult because of the small type and numerous words.

Procedure

Photocopy and enlarge sections of text to focus on the main points and important facts. Cut and place these on separate sheets of paper to assist students who have difficulties with text because they feel overwhelmed.

Language Arts
Choose a story or text selection. Copy and enlarge portions dealing with the main characters and events, and glue them on separate pages. Have students read and discuss main points, then students may choose to read the original text.

Social Studies/Science
Choose a section of text. Copy and enlarge vocabulary and main concepts and glue on separate pages. Have students read and discuss main points. Students may then choose to read the original text.

Math
With pages that have several problems, choose a few to copy, enlarge, and place on a separate page.

Assessment

Evaluate comprehension by discussing the main ideas and using written questions. Students should correctly respond to 80% of the written or discussion questions .

Question-Answer Relationship (QAR)

This strategy helps students to recognize the four possible areas in which answers can be found:

1. Right there—in a single sentence in the text.
2. Putting it together—in several sentences in the text.
3. On my own—in the student's background knowledge.
4. Writer and me—in a combination of information from text and reader's background.

Language Arts

Social Studies

Science

Math

Procedure

Have students read a story, text selection, or math problem. Use questions from the textbook or create questions on your own for students to answer. Determine what information is needed to answer each question. Decide if the information is "right there" stated plainly in one sentence in the text; if it will require reading several questions to answer; if the answer is not in the text but can be answered using students' background information; or if it can be answered by combining background information with information from the text.

Language Arts
Topic: A Short Story
1. Right there: What is the setting?
2. Putting it together: Why was the character upset?
3. On my own: In what situations have you been upset?
4. Writer and me: Is there anyone who reminds you of the character in the story? Who and why?

Social Studies
Topic: Egyptian Religion
1. Right there: Who was the god of the living and dead?
2. Putting it together: What beliefs did people have about Amon-Re?
3. On my own: Why would religion be important to the people?
4. Writer and me: Why would Egyptians prepare so much for the afterlife?

Science
Topic: Erosion
1. Right there: What is erosion?
2. Putting it together: How is erosion related to weathering?
3. On my own: Have you experienced any difficulties dealing with erosion in your life?
4. Writer and me: What areas around you have problems with erosion and what can be done about it?

(continued)

Banikowski & Mehring, 1999; Gunning, 1996; McIntosh & Draper, 1996; Pearson & Johnson, 1978; Raphael, 1982; Swanson & De La Paz, 1998

1: Right there: What is an integer?
2: Putting it together: What types of integers are there?
3: On my own: When would I use negative numbers?
4: Writer and me: How would I balance a checkbook?

Assessment

Check to see if correct responses are given for "Right there" and "Putting it together." If not, refer students back to the text. Use teacher evaluation to assess "On my own" and "Writer and me."

Read Three Times

This is a mathematics strategy used in solving word problems and logic problems. The strength of this strategy is the specific steps used to assist students in determining what is necessary to solve the problem. Once students have used this strategy several times, they should be able to use it without referring to their notes.

Procedure

Students should begin by reading through a word problem quickly. Then they should list words they do not understand. Next, they need to answer the following questions:

- What is the problem asking you to do?
- What do you need to know?
- What is unnecessary information?
- What materials do you need?
- What math operation(s) will you use?

The students should read through the problem at least two more times until they understand. If they still have problems, they should ask for help.

> ### Math
> Problem: The temperature was recorded at 15 degrees C. It rose 8, fell 6, rose 12, and fell 23. What was the temperature after these changes?
> - What is the problem asking you to do? *Asking me to add and subtract to find final temperature.*
> - What do you need to know? *Need to know about integers.*
> - What is unnecessary information? *All information is necessary.*
> - What materials do you need? *No materials needed except paper and pencil.*
> - What math operation(s) will you use? *I will use + and - to solve.*

Assessment

Go through each of the questions in the procedure with the students and see if their responses and final answers are correct. If the answer is incorrect, review each step to determine where the error was made.

Manning, 1999b

SQ3R

Although this strategy takes time, it is very effective in improving comprehension because students are allowed to break text into manageable parts.

Procedure

Begin by teaching students the following steps:

[S]urvey—Look through the chapter that is going to be studied for an overall idea of the topic.

[Q]uestion—Turn each heading into a question.

[R]ead to answer the questions.

[R]ecite—At the end of each section, try to answer the questions without looking back; do not take notes until the entire section is read.

[R]eview what you have read; go over all the questions you asked yourself and try to answer them.

Modeling a previously studied chapter helps students to understand the steps. This is a strategy they can use independently in the future.

Social Studies
S   Egypt's Powerful Kings and Queens
Q   Who were Egypt's God-Kings and why were they called that?
How did Egypt remain in power for 2,000 years?
Who was the Powerful Queen, Great Pharaoh?
Read - Recite answers - Review

Science
S   Moving Water
Q   How do the earth's surfaces affect what happens to water?
How does water cycle through the environment?
What happens to rainwater that runs off?
How can the water level in the ground be changed?
Read - Recite answers - Review

Assessment

Determine student comprehension through evaluation of the questions used for headings, correct answers given, discussion, and teacher observation. Teacher observation should include monitoring the involvement of individual students and their responses. Discussion can be used to determine students' level of comprehension by assessing their responses during the "recite" and "review" part of the strategy.

Gunning, 1996; Robinson, 1961

Teaching Vocabulary

Rather than having students write out vocabulary words and define them using a dictionary, with this strategy students use the context of the literature they are reading to figure out a word's meaning. This strategy can begin as a class activity by writing unknown words on the board and going through the procedures as a group. Eventually, students should be able to create individual lists and follow the procedures on their own.

Procedure

First, students should look through a story or text section and underline or write down unknown words. Next they should predict what they believe to be the meaning of each word based on the context. Finally, discuss these words as a group to determine meaning.

Language Arts
Word: *presumptuous*
Sentence: *She was presumptuous because she said she already had a frame for the winning certificate.*
Predicted meaning: confident, bold

Social Studies
Word: *quarantined*
Sentence: *The immigrants with diseases were quarantined until they were no longer contagious.*
Predicted meaning: kept by themselves

Science
Word: *unsaturated*
Sentence: *The sponge was unsaturated so it was used to clean up the spill.*
Predicted meaning: able to absorb liquid

Assessment

Review predicted meanings. Discussion can be used to determine students' level of comprehension by assessing their responses after reading.

Dole, Sloan, & Trathen, 1995

Text Lookbacks

Often students feel they are not allowed to use their textbooks for studying. Instead they rely on their notes. They need to realize that the textbook is a study guide, and it should be used to clarify or locate information when studying. Once the students have learned this strategy, they can use it on their own.

Procedure

Discuss with students that it is appropriate during studying to "look back" through the textbook to locate information. Begin by modeling skimming for information with the students. It is helpful to begin with short passages and proceed to longer ones. Explain how to use headings and boldfaced words to search for information.

Language Arts/Social Studies/Science
Use the strategy with short sections of text that have questions at the end.

Math
Use the strategy throughout a textbook to review proper operations or necessary information.

Assessment

Answers given to the questions orally or in writing will help determine students' level of comprehension.

Think-Aloud

Think-Aloud can help students to understand the thought processes associated with silent reading. This strategy helps students recognize that they should be thinking about various things related to the text as they read. Students may then be encouraged to use this strategy on their own.

Procedure

Model this strategy by reading a short selection aloud. Students should talk about their thoughts regarding the selection, discussing what they understand and what they may need to learn more about.

Language Arts
While reading a story, ask questions such as, Why is this character acting as he or she is? What may have happened to cause this character to be in this place at this time? What would you do? When and where does the story take place?

Social Studies
While reading about Egypt's kings and queens, ask questions such as, How did they know the statues that appeared to be men were actually of women?

Assessment

Use discussion, tests, quizzes, and teacher questioning. Discussion can be used to determine student's level of comprehension by assessing their responses after reading. Encourage responses from students who appear off task. Students should correctly respond to 80% of the questions during a discussion or given on a quiz or test.

Gunning, 1996

Vocabulary Notebooks

This strategy requires that students keep a notebook with vocabulary words from the text and words assigned by you. Students look up the words in a dictionary or are given definitions, then they write an original sentence using each word. Having the students create their own sentences rather than copying sentences with the vocabulary words ensures that they understand the meaning of each word. This should enhance students' text comprehension by providing a resource for understanding unfamiliar words.

Procedure

Have the students keep a notebook for your class. As you introduce new topics, write vocabulary words on the board and have students copy them in their notebooks. You can give students the definitions or have them look the words up in a glossary or dictionary. Have students use each word in a sentence. If students find additional words they do not know, have them add the words to their vocabulary notebook. The notebooks will be valuable tools as students read and study.

Language Arts
Use with vocabulary from stories and adapt as a grammar notebook (e.g., *preposterous, magnanimous*). Use vocabulary words from the text or create a list of your own.

Social Studies
Use with vocabulary words such as *irrigation, terrain, constitution, latitude,* and *longitude.*

Science
Use with vocabulary such as *lunar, constellation,* or *biology.*

Math
Use with mathematical terms such as *proportion, parallel,* and *quadrilateral.*

Assessment

Use teacher questioning, discussion, and student responses to show understanding of the words. Teacher questioning should involve individual student responses to check for understanding. Discussion can be used to determine students' level of comprehension by assessing their responses to the vocabulary terms.

Bean & Zigmond, 1994

Teaching to Learning Style

Audiotapes

Using audiotapes improves text comprehension for students who have difficulty reading and for students who better comprehend information obtained through auditory means. The strategy allows students individually and in small groups to listen to information several times until they have comprehended the material. This is a strategy that is most useful in areas in which there are long passages of text such as in literature, science, and social studies.

Procedure

Use tapes that have been provided with the text, or have volunteers read and record the text. These tapes can be used with the entire class or with individual students who use headphones during silent reading. Individual students also could check tapes out or use them at a time outside class. The use of adjustable speed recorders is beneficial because readers may slow the tape if the reader is reading too fast.

Language Arts
Use the strategy primarily with stories and poems. If volunteers are taping, ask them to read with expression, and to read any questions that might be associated with the text. This also can be used to reinforce grammar skills by reading over the grammar/usage rules and giving examples on tape.

Social Studies/Science
Use with any text that will benefit the student. It is best to use short tapes and record each section or chapter on a separate tape. Have these available prior to the lesson so students are able to go over the text before it is used in class.

Math
Use with word problems. Additional information can be given on the tape to assist students in choosing the correct method for solving the problems.

Assessment

Determine from teacher questioning, text questions, and discussion whether or not the student is comprehending the text. Teacher questioning and text questions should assist in determining student comprehension. Students should correctly respond to 80% of the questions. Discussion can be used to determine students' comprehension by assessing their responses after reading.

Koskinen, 1995

Combined Reading

Combined reading gives students the opportunity to receive information in both visual (silent reading) and auditory (reading aloud) manners.

Procedure

First, assign a passage for silent reading. After a sufficient amount of time, instruct the students to begin reading aloud in a specific arrangement. This may involve students reading aloud in small groups, individuals reading in a group setting, or you modeling reading aloud. Tactile learners may be instructed to use a bookmark to follow along with the reading of the text.

Language Arts

Social Studies

Science

Math

Language Arts
Topic: Poem
After students have read the poem silently, assign partners to alternate reading lines or verses to each other. Regroup and discuss the poem with the whole class.

Social Studies
Topic: Egyptian Pyramids
After silent reading, reread the selection by calling on individual students randomly. At the end of the selection, discuss and ask questions.

Science
Topic: Cells
After reading silently, divide the class into four groups. Assign a strong reader in each group and have each reader read aloud to his or her group. Allow time for small-group discussion before bringing the class together.

Assessment

Through discussion and teacher questioning determine the level of comprehension from the group. Individuals may be regrouped and allowed to reread as necessary. Teacher questioning should involve individual student responses to check for understanding. Discussion can be used to determine students' level of comprehension by assessing their responses. If students do not answer correctly, refer them back to the text.

Bean & Zigmond, 1994

Creative Dramatics

This strategy is a creative, exciting way to motivate students while helping them recognize the main idea they will be studying. The strategy is an interesting way for students to understand why a character may act a certain way, and it can be used with a variety of situations.

Procedure

Decide what main point you would like to cover. This may be related to character or historical motivation or actions. Before introducing the reading, present situations to the students that they will be familiar with and that are related to the main point of the reading. Choose students to participate in acting out the situation and have them make decisions regarding what they would do. Assist students as necessary as they prepare the "acting" situation. Guide students by presenting questions that will lead them to realize why a person might respond a certain way. After this has been done, students will read the story or text and discuss the relationship between the creative drama activity and the reading.

Language Arts

Topic: *Julius Caesar*
Ask three students to role-play. One would be the new school president; the other two would be his or her friends who are unsure of the way the president is using his or her power. One friend would be afraid that the school would suffer due to the president's abuse of power. Ask the students to decide what they would do, including what action would be taken if the president refused to listen to their concerns.

Assessment

Through discussion, teacher observation, and questioning, determine if students are able to state the main idea in the lesson they are covering. Teacher observation should include monitoring the involvement of individual students and their responses. Teacher questioning and discussion can be used to determine students' level of comprehension by assessing their responses. Encourage responses from students who appear off task. If students do not respond correctly, provide additional information and refer them back to the text in order to reexamine the passage.

Kaplan, 1997

Draw a Picture

This strategy is simple yet gives a way for students to be successful. Because many students learn visually, this strategy helps them to organize and conceptualize what a text is about.

Procedure

After students have read a story or passage, ask them to draw a simple picture of what the text is about. Give guidelines for the pictures by having students answer the following questions in their drawings: What is the setting? Who are the characters? When did the story take place? What is happening? If vocabulary is a problem, the students may label items or actions in the picture. After they have drawn their pictures, they should write a short summary paragraph. The short paragraph allows you to see if the student really understands the text.

Language Arts

Read a short story and ask students to think about setting, character, and events. Have them picture a scene in their mind that tells about the story. Ask students to draw a picture (stick figures are fine), label it, and write a summary paragraph. For example, students could illustrate a story about a girl who is always on the phone so her parents limit her to three calls at three minutes each day. She is angry until a boy calls to ask her out and she realizes that he had been trying to call her for weeks, but the phone was always busy.

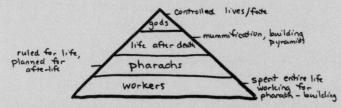

Social Studies/Science

Read a short selection and ask students to think about the information presented. Have them picture a scene in their mind that tells about the selection. Ask students to draw a picture (stick figures are fine), label it, and write a summary paragraph. For example, in social studies, students could depict the unique aspects of life in Egypt: the gods they worshiped, belief in life after death, the pharaohs who ruled the country, and the workers who spent their lives building pyramids and other things for their leaders.

In science, students could depict the three states of matter: solids, liquids, and gases. Each of these have their own properties.

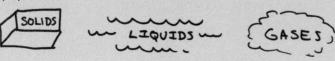

Banikowski & Mehring, 1999; J. Pederson (e-mail to author, October 23, 1999)

(continued)

Math

Students could visually represent a word problem. For example, a boy purchases three drinks at $.90 each and two large popcorns at $1.25 each. He divides the total cost with his two friends. How much will each of the three have to pay?

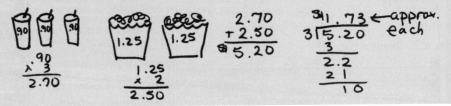

Assessment

Use teacher evaluation of the drawing, evaluation of summary paragraph, and discussion to determine if the main ideas have been addressed. Teacher evaluation should include reviewing drawings with students to see if the drawings correctly conceptualize what the text is about. Discussion can be used to determine students' level of comprehension by assessing their responses. If the drawing does not represent the text correctly, provide additional information and refer the student back to the text in order to reexamine the information that should be included in the drawing.

Highlight Text

This strategy helps students focus on the most important points or items in a text. The highlighter colors help visual learners notice facts and important points in a text.

Procedure

Set a certain number of textbooks aside for students who need assistance identifying the most important points or items in a text. Go through these texts with a highlighter to identify important information.

Language Arts
Use the strategy with stories, poems, or grammar; highlight main ideas, characters, and vocabulary.

Social Studies/Science
Use with any section of text; highlight vocabulary terms, names, places, and main concepts.

Math
Highlight words that identify which operation to use in solving a problem.

Assessment

Use teacher evaluation, discussion, and a quiz or test to determine comprehension. Teacher observation should include monitoring the involvement of individual students and their responses. Discussion can be used to determine students' level of comprehension by assessing their responses after reading. Encourage responses from students who appear off task. Students should correctly respond to 80% of the questions during a discussion or given on a quiz. Assist students who need to continue to read aloud by pairing them with other readers.

Small, 1996

Journal

This strategy is helpful in assessing comprehension and allowing students to think through the information that has been taught. This is also useful in getting students to think about a theme such as "Life is not fair—agree or disagree" before reading Steinbeck's *The Red Pony*.

Procedure

The first step in this strategy involves giving a prompt that is instructional, contextual, reflective, or other. For example, when studying Egypt, ask the students, What type of person would you have wanted to be if you had lived in Ancient Egypt? Allow the students 5 to 8 minutes to write about the prompt. Students turn in their journals, and you are able to determine if their responses show comprehension of the material that was covered.

Language Arts
Ask students, What is the setting in this story? What feelings is the main character expressing? How would you react in this situation?

Social Studies
Ask, What type of person would you like to be if you had lived in Ancient Egypt? Why?

Science
Ask, How are sounds produced? How do stirring and temperature affect dissolving?

Math
Ask, How would you tell someone to solve the following problem: $3x + 4x = 35$?

Assessment

Use teacher observation and individual evaluation (written or oral) to determine if students are comprehending the text.

DiPillo & Sovchik, 1997; Vacca & Vacca, 1989

Radio Reading

This strategy is a simple form of oral reading that gives students many ways to learn information. Students are exposed to visual, auditory, and tactile learning.

Procedure

After students have read a selection independently, have individual students reread sections aloud. During this, students who are not reading aloud close their books and listen to the reader, concentrating on meaning. Afterward, students summarize the text, referring back to the text if necessary.

Language Arts
Use the strategy with stories, poems, or text selections. Assign students to read specific passages and have their place marked so they will be prepared when it is their turn.

Social Studies/Science
Use with text selections. It is preferable to have one student read through an entire selection before changing students.

Math
Use with word problems.

Assessment

Using discussion and student summaries, determine if students have comprehended the overall concept of the material. Discussion and student summaries can be used to determine students' level of comprehension by assessing their responses after reading. Students' responses should communicate the main idea of the text. If they do not, refer them back to the text or have other students share their summaries.

Vacca & Vacca, 1989

Visual Adjuncts

Often visual adjuncts to text are overlooked and student comprehension of these visuals is assumed when it should not be. These resources are particularly helpful for visual learners in helping to clarify concepts that are being studied.

Procedure

During text instruction, discuss in detail the tables, charts, graphs, and photos to assist students in clarifying, enriching, or reinforcing concepts that are discussed in the text. When appropriate, students can construct their own visuals to assist with comprehension.

Language Arts

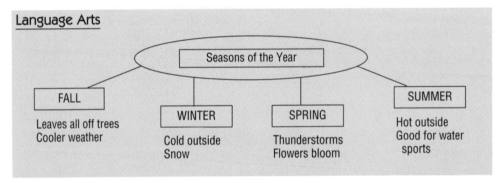

Social Studies

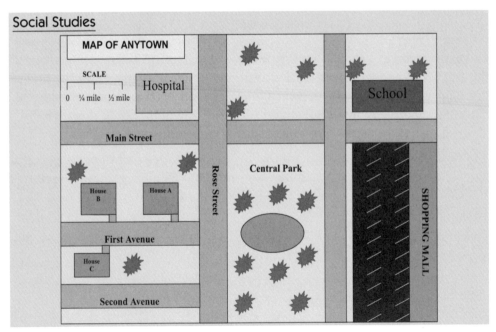

Craig & Yore, 1996

76

Science

Solid	Liquid	Gas
Ice	Water	Steam
Book	Peroxide	Carbon Monoxide
Pencil	Alcohol	Oxygen

Math

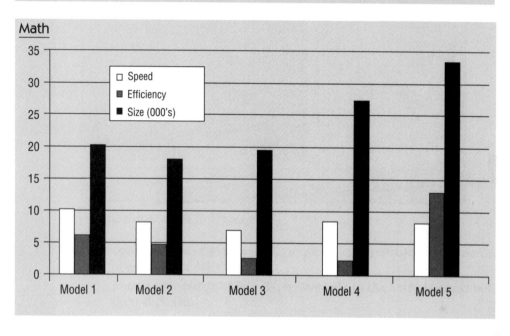

Assessment

Use discussion, quizzes, tests, and teacher questioning to determine understanding of the visual adjuncts. Teacher observation should include monitoring the involvement of individual students and their responses. Discussion can be used to determine students' level of comprehension by assessing their responses after reading. Students should correctly respond to 80% of the questions posed in a discussion or given on a quiz.

References

Aarnoutse, C., & Brand-Gruwel, S. (1997). Improving reading comprehension strategies through listening. *Educational Studies, 23*(2), 209–227.

Alvermann, D.E., Young, J.P., Weaver, D., Hinchman, K.A., Moore, D.W., Phelps, S.F., Thrash, E.C., & Zalewski, P. (1996). Middle and high school students' perceptions of how they experience text-based discussions: A multicase study. *Reading Research Quarterly, 31,* 244–267.

Aronson, E. (1997). *The jigsaw classroom: Building cooperation in the classroom* (2nd ed.). Thousand Oaks, CA: Sage.

Arreaga-Mayer, C. (1998). Increasing active student responding and improving academic performance through classwide peer tutoring. *Intervention in School and Clinic, 34*(2), 89–94, 117.

Banikowski, A.K., & Mehring, T.A. (1999). Strategies to enhance memory based on brain-research. *Focus on Exceptional Children, 32*(2), 1–16.

Barrentine, S.J. (1996). Engaging with reading through interactive read-alouds. *The Reading Teacher, 50,* 36–43.

Bean, R.M., & Zigmond, N. (1994). Adapted use of social studies textbooks in elementary classrooms: Views of classroom teachers. *Remedial and Special Education, 15*(4), 216–226.

Bromley, K., & Modlo, M. (1997). Using cooperative learning to improve reading and writing in language arts. *Reading and Writing Quarterly, 13*(1), 21–35.

Bryant, D.P., Ugel, N., Thompson, S., & Hamff, A. (1999). Instructional strategies for content-area reading instruction. *Intervention in School and Clinic, 34*(5), 293–302.

Buehl, D. (1997). Loud and clear. *The Reading Room* [Online]. Available: http://www.weac.org/News/SEPT97/read.htm.

Bulgren, J., & Scanlon, D. (1998). Instructional routines and learning strategies that promote understanding of content area concepts. *Journal of Adolescent & Adult Literacy, 41,* 292–302.

Caverly, D.C., Mandeville, T.F., & Nicholson, S.A. (1995). PLAN: A study-reading strategy for informational text. *Journal of Adolescent & Adult Literacy, 39,* 190–199.

Cochran, J.A. (1993). Reading in the content areas for junior high and high school. Boston: Allyn & Bacon.

Craig, M.T., & Yore, L.D. (1996). Middle school students' awareness of strategies for resolving comprehension difficulties in science reading. *Journal of Research and Development in Education, 29*(4), 226–238.

Delquadri, J.C., Greenwood, C.R., Stretton, K., & Hall, R.V. (1983). The peer tutoring spelling game: A classroom procedure for increasing opportunity to respond and spelling performance. *Education and Treatment of Children, 6*(3), 225–239.

DiPillo, M.L., & Sovchik, R. (1997). Exploring middle graders' mathematical thinking through journals. *Mathematics Teaching in the Middle School, 2*(5), 308–314.

Dole, J.A., Brown, K.J., & Woodrow, T. (1996). The effects of strategy instruction on the comprehension performance of at-risk students. *Reading Research Quarterly, 31,* 62–88.

Dole, J.A., Sloan, C., & Trathen, W. (1995). Teaching vocabulary within the context of literature. *Journal of Reading, 38*(6), 452–460.

Emery, D.W. (1996). Helping readers comprehend stories from the characters' perspectives. *The Reading Teacher, 49,* 534–541.

Fuentes, P. (1998). Reading comprehension in mathematics. *Clearing House, 72*(2), 81–88.

Gunning, T.G. (1996). *Creating reading instruction for all children* (2nd ed.). Boston: Allyn & Bacon.

Hendrix, J.C. (1999). Connecting cooperative learning and social studies. *Clearing House, 73*(1), 57–60.

Herber, H.L. (1978). *Teaching reading in the content areas.* Englewood Cliffs, NJ: Prentice-Hall.

Ivey, G. (1999a). A multicase study in the middle school: Complexities among young adolescent readers. *Reading Research Quarterly, 34,* 172–192.

Ivey, G. (1999b). Reflections on teaching struggling middle school readers. *Journal of Adolescent & Adult Literacy, 42,* 372–381.

Jeffrey, C.R. (1997). K-W-L learning journals: A way to encourage reflection. *Journal of Adolescent & Adult Literacy, 40,* 392–393.

Kaplan, J. (1997). Acting up across the curriculum: Using creative dramatics to explore adolescent literature. *ALAN Review, 24*(3), 42–46.

Katims, D.S., & Harris, S. (1997). Improving the reading comprehension of middle school students in inclusive classrooms. *Journal of Adolescent & Adult Literacy, 41,* 116–123.

Koskinen, P. (1995). *Have you heard any good books lately? Encouraging shared reading at home with books and audiotapes.* Athens, GA: National Reading Research Center. (ERIC Document Reproduction Service No. ED385827)

Lamme, L.L., & Beckett, C. *Whole language in an elementary school library media center.* Syracuse, NY: ERIC Clearinghouse on Information Resources. (ERIC Document Reproduction Service No. ED346874)

Manning, M. (1999a). Reading across the curriculum. *Teaching Pre-K–8, 29* (5), 83–85.

Manning, M. (1999b). Building reading skills in math. *Teaching Pre-K–8, 29*(7), 85–86.

Manzo, A.V. (1969). The ReQuest procedure. *Journal of Reading, 13*(2), 123–126, 163.

McIntosh, M.E., & Draper, R.J. (1995). Applying the question-answer relationship strategy in mathematics. *Journal of Adolescent & Adult Literacy, 39,* 120–131.

McIntosh, M.E., & Draper, R.J. (1996). Using the question-answer relationship strategy to improve students' reading of mathematics texts. *Clearing House, 69*(3), 154–162.

Muth, D.K. (1997). Using cooperative learning to improve reading and writing in mathematical problem solving. *Reading and Writing Quarterly, 13*(1), 71–82.

Nesbit, C.R., & Rogers, C.A. (1997). Using cooperative learning to improve reading and writing in science. *Reading and Writing Quarterly, 13*(1), 53–70.

Ogle, D.M. (1986). K-W-L: A teaching model that develops active reading of expository text. *The Reading Teacher, 39,* 564–570.

Ogle, D.M. (1994). Assessment: Helping our students see their learning. *Teaching Pre-K-8, 25*(2), 100–101.

Palincsar, A.S. (1984). The quest for meaning from expository text: A teacher-guided journey. In G. Duffy, L.R. Roehler, & J.D. Mason (Eds.), *Comprehension instruction: Perspectives and suggestions* (pp. 251–264). New York: Longman.

Pearson, P.D., & Johnson, D.D. (1978). *Teaching reading comprehension.* New York: Holt, Rinehart & Winston.

Raphael, T.E. (1982). Question-answering strategies for children. *The Reading Teacher, 36,* 186–190.

Robinson, F. (1961). *Effective study.* New York: Harper and Row.

Shanahan, S., & Shanahan, T. (1997). Character perspective charting: Helping children to develop a more complete conception of story. *The Reading Teacher, 50,* 668–677.

Slavin, R.E. (1988). Cooperative learning and student achievement. *Educational Leadership, 46*(2), 31–33.

Small, D. (1996). Navigating large bodies of text. *IBM Systems Journal, 35*(3 & 4).

Swanson, P.N., & De La Paz, S. (1998). Teaching effective comprehension strategies to students with learning and reading disabilities. *Intervention in School and Clinic, 33*(4), 209–218.

Vacca, R.T., & Vacca, J.L. (1989). *Content area reading* (3rd ed.). New York: HarperCollins.

Vallecorsa, A.L., & deBettencourt, L.U. (1997). Using a mapping procedure to teach reading and writing skills to middle grade students with learning disabilities. *Education and Treatment of Children, 20*(2), 173–188.

Vaughn, S., & Klingner, J.K. (1999). Teaching reading comprehension through collaborative strategic reading. *Intervention in School and Clinic, 34*(5), 284–292.

Warren, J.S., & Flynt, S.W. (1995). Children with attention deficit disorder: Diagnosis and prescription of reading skill deficits. *Reading Improvement, 32*(2), 105–110.

Winograd, K., & Higgins, K.M. (1995). Writing, reading, and talking mathematics: One interdisciplinary possibility. *The Reading Teacher, 48*, 310–318.